Text by Lois Rock

Illustrations copyright © 2007 Sophie Allsopp

This edition copyright © 2007 Lion Hudson

The moral rights of the author and illustrator
have been asserted

A Lion Children's Book
an imprint of
Lion Hudson plc
Wilkinson House, Jordan Hill Road,
Oxford OX2 8DR, England
www.lionhudson.com
ISBN 978 0 7459 4956 7

First edition 2007
1 3 5 7 9 10 8 6 4 2 0

Typeset in 18/24 Caslon Old Face BT
Printed and bound in China

The First CHRISTMAS

Lois Rock

Illustrated by Sophie Allsopp

LION
CHILDREN'S

Long ago, a girl named Mary lived in Nazareth.

She believed in God, and she wanted to please God in all she did.

She was dreaming of getting married, and already it was planned that she should marry Joseph.

But she had never imagined that she would see an angel.

Yet there, right in front of her, was the angel Gabriel; and the angel had a message from God.

'Don't be afraid,' said Gabriel. 'I have good news. God has chosen you to be the mother of a child. You will name him Jesus.'

'But that can't be true!' replied Mary. 'I'm not even married yet.'

'God will make this come true,' said the angel. 'The child will be God's son.'

In her heart, Mary knew it was right to do what God wanted.

Joseph knew for sure that he was doing the right thing.

'Darling Mary,' he said, 'I want us to be married.

'Our families want us to be married.

'And in a dream, an angel said to me that God wants us to be married.

'So now we will go to my home town of Bethlehem together.

'We will put our names on the list of taxpayers together.
'We will be husband and wife, together for ever.'

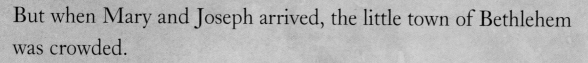

But when Mary and Joseph arrived, the little town of Bethlehem was crowded.

The inn was full.

The only place left for Mary and Joseph was a low-roofed cave where an ox munched hay and the little donkey stamped and shuffled.

'I think my baby is going to born tonight,' said Mary, sounding worried.

'We will be safe and warm here,' said Joseph. 'And look: the manger is just the right size for a cradle.'

Out on the hillside, the shepherds huddled by the sheepfold.
  'What a job,' grumbled one, 'having to stay out here in the cold and dark with jackals on the prowl for a tasty sheep.'

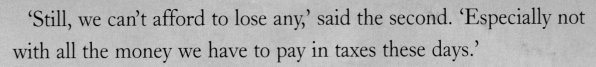

'Still, we can't afford to lose any,' said the second. 'Especially not with all the money we have to pay in taxes these days.'

'I blame the emperor,' said the third. 'If we had a proper king of our own, things might be better.'

All at once, the sky exploded into brightness.

'Good news!' called a voice, and an angel stood in front of them. 'Tonight, in Bethlehem, a child has been born. He is lying in a manger, but truly he is a king. God has sent him to put everything in the world to rights.'

All around, a hundred thousand angels danced through the glittering sky.

'Glory to God in heaven!' they sang.

'Peace on earth!'

Then, just as suddenly, the sky went dark.

'Let's go to Bethlehem,' cried the shepherds. 'Let's find out
if this is true.'

In the lamplit cave they found Mary and Joseph.

And there was the baby Jesus, lying in a manger.

From far away in the east, wise and learned men came riding.
They came to the city of Jerusalem and began asking questions.
'We are following a bright new star,' they explained.

'It is a sign that a king has been born. We have come
to bring him gifts. Do you know where we can find him?'
The king in Jerusalem was Herod. He was only a servant
of the emperor, but he liked his palaces and his power.
He demanded to see the men.

'I have asked the wise and learned men in Jerusalem all about your king,' he said. 'Long ago, God promised to send our people a king – the greatest king of all will be born in Bethlehem.'

Herod leaned closer.

'I want you to go and find him,' he said. 'Then come and tell me where he is.'

The star led the way to a house in Bethlehem.

They went inside and found Mary and her baby, and they gave him royal gifts:

Gold and frankincense and myrrh.

It wasn't long before angels were warning of danger ahead.

'Hurry,' an angel told the wise men in a dream. 'Herod wants to harm the baby king. Go home by a different road.'

'Hurry,' an angel told Joseph in a dream. 'Herod wants to harm little Jesus. Go to Egypt – you will not be safe while Herod is alive.'

At long last, the little family returned to Nazareth.

Mary and Joseph and the angels had kept Jesus safe.

Now he would grow up to do the work for which he had been born.

And those who learned to love and to follow him would have Christmases for always.